Randy Moss: The Inspiring Story of One of Football's Star Wide Receivers

An Unauthorized Biography

D1715018

By: Clayton Geoffreys

Table of Contents

Foreword

Randy Moss achieved a lot over the course of his professional football career. At the time of this writing, he holds the NFL's single-season touchdown reception record, and the single-season touchdown reception record for a rookie. While he never won a Super Bowl (both appearances his teams made resulted in losses), Moss was consistently selected for Pro Bowls and led the NFL in receiving touchdowns five times. Many regard Randy Moss as one of the greatest wide receivers of all time. Thank you for purchasing *Randy Moss: The Inspiring Story of One of Football's Star Wide Receivers*. In this unauthorized biography, we will learn Randy Moss' incredible life story and impact on the game of football. Hope you enjoy and if you do, please do not forget to leave a review!

Also, check out my website at claytongeoffreys.com to join my exclusive list where I let you know about my latest books. To thank you for your purchase, you can go to my site to download a free copy of *33 Life Lessons: Success Principles, Career Advice & Habits of Successful People.* In the book, you'll learn from some of the greatest thought leaders of different industries on what it takes to become successful and how to live a great life.

Cheers,

Clayton Geoffreys

Visit me at www.claytongeoffreys.com

Introduction

Some people just have the gift. They are born with the ability to be bigger, faster, and stronger than normal human beings. They use that gift in the athletic field of their choosing and dominate the field.

Jim Thorpe was the first American multi-sport hero. He started out by winning two Olympic gold medals in the pentathlon and decathlon. He went on to play professional football, baseball, and basketball. Thorpe is widely considered the best athlete of the first half of the twentieth century, if for no other reason than he was not just good at four sports, but he *dominated* in all of them.

As World War II approached, African American athletes began to get their chance to participate at major universities across the country. Jackie Robinson would eventually break the color line in baseball, but first, he was a star at UCLA. He was the first athlete in the history of the university to letter in four sports.

Robinson obviously played baseball, but he also lettered in basketball, football, and track for the Bruins.

The 1950s saw possibly the greatest athlete in the history of two separate sports. Jim Brown is arguably the best running back in the history of the NFL, but he was also considered to be the best *lacrosse* player ever. And while he was at Syracuse University, he also lettered in basketball.

Finally, there was probably the greatest athlete there ever was: Bo Jackson. While he was in high school in Alabama, Jackson received an astounding 16 varsity letters, which means that he lettered in four sports all four years he was in high school. He is known for football and baseball, but he also played basketball and ran track, and he was remarkably talented at *all* of it. He set the Alabama state record in both the high jump and triple jump. Jackson went on to play both football and baseball professionally. He was a dominant running back for the Raiders and an all-star outfielder for the Royals and White Sox.

Randy Moss was cut from the same cloth as Jackson, Brown, Robinson, and Thorpe. While in high school, Moss was twice named the best football player in the state of West Virginia, but he was also a two-time West Virginia Player of the Year in basketball. He ran track for one season and won the 100- and 200-meter state championships. There was seemingly nothing Moss could not do.

Moss was born in Rand, West Virginia, to a single mother. His mother worked hard to ensure that he and his two siblings had a roof over their heads. The family was poor, and Moss used sports as his outlet in life.

It was also sports that helped Moss form friendships that would take him through high school. He met Bobby Howard and Sam Singleton Jr. through his first baseball team. Singleton's father, Sam Sr., would coach all three boys until they reached high school, and Moss latched onto Sam Sr. as that missing father figure in his life.

Rand was predominantly African American, but the town next to it, Belle, was mostly white. Both towns fed into Dupont High School, which was located in Belle. African American students only made up 3% of the population of the high school, but nonetheless, they were the most visible athletes in the school.

Dupont High School had a number of racial-related issues to overcome while Moss was there, especially from a group of students in an area dubbed "Redneck Alley." The students in this area constantly harassed Moss and his friends. The taunting got worse for Moss when he started dating Libby Offutt, who was white. During Moss's senior year, the young couple welcomed a daughter, Sydney.

On the field and court, Moss was the most dominant athlete the state of West Virginia ever produced. He led his football team to two state championships and was twice named the top player in the state. Along with future NBA star Jason Williams, Moss led his basketball team to the state championship game before losing. During his senior season, he averaged more than 30 points and 10 rebounds a game. He tried track for a year and won the state titles in the 100- and 200-meter races.

It was no surprise that Moss was recruited by nearly every college football team in America. He narrowed his choices down to three schools: Florida, Tennessee, and Notre Dame. But in reality, there was only one school for Moss—Notre Dame. During his senior year, he signed with the Irish.

As his fame grew, so did the resentment of the white students at Dupont. During his senior year, Moss was involved in a racially motivated fight where a white student was sent to the hospital.

Moss was arrested and originally charged with a felony. He had the charges reduced to a misdemeanor and had to spend 30 days in prison. The judge allowed him to attend his freshman year in college and then return to West Virginia to complete his sentence the following summer.

Despite the reduced charges, the damage was done to Moss's reputation and status at Notre Dame. The university revoked his admission and he was not allowed to play there. Irish coach Lou Holtz called his friend at Florida State, Bobby Bowden, who agreed to let Moss enroll at the school and play football on the condition that he stayed out of trouble, and he had to redshirt for his freshman season.

While redshirting at Florida State, Moss routinely torched one of the best defenses in the country. He had the second-fastest 40-yard dash time in the history of the school, behind only Deion Sanders.

When Moss returned to West Virginia following his freshman year to serve his 30-day sentence, he failed a drug test at his intake. The judge revoked the terms of his plea agreement and put him in prison, awaiting a hearing. Moss spent the first seven days of his prison time in solitary confinement. He was only 19 years old.

It appeared as though Moss was going to be another tragic story of a star athlete who did not make it because of his run-ins with the law. But the small but vocal African American community in West Virginia rallied around Moss and convinced the judge to give him another opportunity.

Moss was sentenced to 60 days in prison, including time served. This would allow him to enroll in a college and be able to play football in the fall, but what college would take him?

Despite his love/hate relationship with the state of West Virginia, it was Marshall University in Huntington that gave Moss the opportunity he was looking for. Marshall was an FCS school, which allowed Moss to be eligible to play immediately.

In two seasons at Marshall, Moss dominated the competition. He was twice named an All-American and helped lead the Thunder Herd to the 1996 Division 1AA National Championship and an undefeated season. He ended his career at Marshall with 3,529 receiving yards and 54 touchdowns in 28 games.

Coming into the 1998 NFL Draft, Moss was clearly one of the best players on the board, but concerns over his youthful off-the-field issues hurt his draft prospects. Because of those concerns, he dropped all the way down to the 21st pick, where he was selected by the Minnesota Vikings.

But being in Minnesota could not have been better for Moss. The team had a strong leader in coach Dennis Green and a veteran team led by fellow receiver Cris Carter.

Moss proved his worth during his first season in the league. Minnesota had the number one offense in the NFL and went 15-1. He set the rookie record for receiving touchdowns with 17. The Vikings made it all the way to the NFC Championship game but lost in a stunner to the Atlanta Falcons. After the season, Moss was named the Offensive Rookie of the Year, first-team All-Pro, and made his first Pro Bowl.

During his first three seasons in Minnesota, Moss led the league in touchdown receptions twice, made the Pro Bowl three times, was the Pro Bowl's Most Valuable Player, and was first-team All-Pro twice. Minnesota went back to the NFC Championship game for a second time in Moss's third season only to lose to the New York Giants.

After three seasons, Moss signed an eight-year, $75-million contract extension with the Vikings. But by then, the wheels had started to come off in Minnesota. Green was fired near the end of the 2001 season and replaced by Mike Tice. The team struggled despite Moss's outstanding production.

After the 2004 season, Moss was traded to the Oakland Raiders. His time in Oakland was just plain awful. The team was terrible, and at times, Moss just did not want to play. During his two seasons with the Raiders, Moss only caught 11 touchdowns.

Finally, the Raiders decided to part ways with Moss and traded him to the New England Patriots prior to the 2007 season. With Tom Brady throwing him the ball and Bill Belichick leading the team, Moss had a resurgence and one of the best seasons ever put up by the wide receiver and his team.

Moss broke the receiving touchdown record set by Jerry Rice with his 23 TDS in 2007. The Patriots ended the regular season at 16-0, the only team in the history of the NFL to accomplish that feat.

For the first time in his career, Moss made it to the Super Bowl. The Patriots were on the verge of history but got knocked off by the New York Giants, 17-14, in the Super Bowl. Moss did catch a touchdown in the loss, but he missed out on a perfect season and a ring.

Moss had two more productive seasons in New England before things went bad for him again. He was looking for a contract extension and made his desires public. In doing so, he broke the cardinal rule of the Patriots—don't tell anyone outside the organization what you're thinking.

Midway through the 2010 season, Moss was traded back to the Vikings. He lasted four games before the Vikings cut him for refusing to speak to the media. He was picked up by Tennessee, but that was a disaster, as he only caught six passes in eight games.

After the 2010 season, Moss quietly retired. But in 2012, he would return for one season with the San Francisco 49ers. He played a lesser role for the 49ers but showed great leadership on a young team that valued his mentorship. The 49ers made it all the way to the Super Bowl, but once again, Moss was denied his ring, this time by the Baltimore Ravens.

Moss once again retired from football and headed into television, a new arena he also excelled at. After his retirement, he worked for Fox Sports, and most recently, ESPN on their *Sunday NFL Countdown* and *Monday Night Countdown*. He was inducted into the Pro Football Hall of Fame in 2018.

Randy Moss is easily one of the greatest receivers the NFL has ever seen. During his 14-year career, he had more than 1,000 yards in a season 10 times and more than 10 touchdowns 9 times. He still holds the record for most touchdown receptions in a season and is second on the NFL's all-time list for receiving touchdowns.

At times, the controversies that surrounded Moss off the field overshadowed what he did on the field. But there is no denying that when he was on, there was no one better than Randy Moss.

Chapter 1: Childhood & High School

Prior to every prime-time game, the hosts run through the starters on offense and defense for each team. The player tells the audience their name and the college they attended. It has been done thousands of times on television, and it gives the players a chance to shout out their college. It is a simple act, but not for Randy Moss.

Later in his career, when he started playing for the New England Patriots, rather than telling people that he had attended Marshall University, Randy Moss told the audience that he came from "Rand University."

Most viewers simply believed that the star receiver was using the name as a play on his own name and that it was just another way to differentiate himself from other players. The reality of it was much more complicated.

The reference to Rand University was a shout-out to Moss's hometown of Rand, West Virginia—not so much the town itself, but a nod to those athletes who were just as gifted as Moss but were unable to make it out. The ones who stood outside the only business in town, a 7-Eleven convenience store, and drank every afternoon.

For Moss, it was his way of showing that he remembered who he was and where he came from. It was also his way of showing all of those people back in West Virginia that they too can find a way out, just like he did.

The state of West Virginia has always felt isolated, even from its outset. The area which now comprises the state was part of the state of Virginia until the start of the Civil War. When Virginia succeeded from the Union, the western part of the state sought to become a separate entity from Virginia rather than join the Confederacy.

There was always a conflict between the eastern and western parts of the state. The east had large plantations and was significantly wealthier. The west was nestled into the Appalachian Mountains and was composed mostly of hardscrabble family farms. So, after Virginia decided to leave the union, the counties that made up West Virginia chose to leave the state of Virginia and in 1863, West Virginia became a state. The vote to leave Virginia was as much an anti-slavery vote as it was a vote against the elites of Eastern Virginia.

West Virginia has always been poor. In fact, it has the fifth-highest poverty rate in America. It also ranks in the bottom five in education, health care, childhood poverty, and most citizens who have food insecurities.[i] Throughout its history, the state has also been exploited for its natural resources. At first, it was salt, then limestone, and then in the late 1800s, coal was found in the mountains.

Just a short drive southwest from the state capital of Charleston is the town of Rand, West Virginia. The town is unincorporated, which means that it does not have a town government of its own. Its population of around 1,000 people is predominantly African American.

And this is where Randy Moss is from. He was born on February 13, 1977, to Maxine Moss and Randy Pratt. Shortly after, Pratt left the family, and Moss's mother was forced to raise him and his two siblings on her own.

"By me being raised without a father, I did not know how to be a father," Moss said. "So, throughout the years of me learning, watching, reading, that's how I became a dad. The only thing I wanted was to give my children everything—or access to everything—that I did not have. It's not about the money. It's about the time that you put into your kids."[ii]

Maxine Moss worked a series of odd jobs, including working in a daycare center in Rand where she would bring Randy with her to help calm the young children.

When he was old enough, Moss would walk around with pacifiers and any time one of the babies started to cry, he would be there with a pacifier to help calm them down.

Besides his mother, the other constant in Moss's life was the church. His mother made sure that the family made it to church every Sunday, as well as weekday mass on both Wednesday and Friday.

The town of Rand only had one store, a 7-Eleven, and did not have a single streetlight. But what it did have was poverty. And there was plenty of that to go around.

"We didn't know what it meant to be poor," Donnie Jones, a Rand resident and Moss's friend and current manager said. "We just thought it was natural. The way we were growing up was the way we were growing up. Nobody had money so we didn't know the value of money. All we knew was we had each other. Playing sports, that's what we thought you did."[iii]

It was through sports that Moss met the friends that he would carry with him throughout the rest of his life. It would also present him with the father figure that he was lacking in his own life. When Moss first started playing baseball, he was on a team with Bobbie Howard and Sam Singleton Jr. The three boys would form an unbreakable bond that would last all throughout high school and beyond.

Singleton's father, Sam Sr., was the team's coach. He stepped in and helped Moss become better at sports and also tried his best to guide him in life. In a strange twist of fate that defies the odds, all three friends— from a town of less than 1,000 people—would eventually play professional sports.

Moss, of course, played in the NFL, as did Howard, who was a linebacker with the Bears for three seasons. Singleton Jr. was drafted by the Milwaukee Brewers in the seventh round of the MLB Draft but was subsequently thrown off the team when he failed a drug test.

The three young friends stuck together, moving from baseball to football and finally to basketball. They became inseparable, both on and off the field. To pass the time when they were not playing organized games, they created their own football game called "razzle-dazzle." It would be this backyard game that helped to create the Randy Moss that the NFL would come to know.

Essentially, razzle-dazzle is a combination of football, rugby, and kill the carrier. The rules are simple: you can throw the ball in any direction you want and once you're down, you lose possession. If you score, you keep the ball until the other team stops you. The idea is to be evasive and keep running as fast as you can. It became the Randy Moss way.

"You learn how to block, you learn how to run, you learn how to cheat, and you learn how to live, man," Howard said of the game.[iv]

The friends would play until the sun went down and retire to Singleton's backyard, so his father could keep an eye on them. They lovingly began calling the yard "the shed," and to this day, Moss still returns there whenever he is back in Rand.

By the time the three friends arrived in high school, they were already local legends for their athletic ability, especially Moss. But Rand did not have a high school, so Moss would be attending Dupont High School. It was only located a mile away from his home, but it was in the prominently white town of Belle.

According to the 2020 U.S. Census Report, white residents make up nearly 94% of the population of West Virginia, while African American residents make up slightly less than 4%. At Dupont High School, the African American population was even less than the state average, with only 3% of the school's students being black.

Belle and Rand were like two separate worlds, despite sharing both a border and a high school. Many of the white students at Dupont held deep-seated racist views of the African American students and were not shy about sharing those views aloud. The white students were especially resentful of the African American athletes, believing that they got more attention than they deserved and special treatment.

During his four years in high school, Moss was involved in a number of racially charged fights, including one during his senior year that nearly derailed his entire future.

Despite the racial tension at the school, Moss excelled on the fields and courts. During his sophomore and junior seasons, he led the Dupont football team to back-to-back state championships. Moss, of course, played receiver, but he also played safety, returned punts and kicks, and was the punter and kicker. It seemed there wasn't anything he couldn't do.[v]

People who know Randy say that his best sport might have been baseball. He played center field for Dupont and routinely patrolled the outfield, taking away extra-base hits from opponents. During his sophomore season, Moss decided that he would go out for the track team. In his only season in track, he won the West Virginia state titles in both the 100- and 200-meter dashes. There seemed to be nothing that Randy Moss couldn't do.

But there's more. When he was not running track, winning state titles in football, or taking away doubles in baseball, Moss was a dominant basketball player. But he was not the only one on his team.

Moss started playing football with Jason Williams when they were both in fourth grade. Williams was the quarterback and Moss was, well, a receiver. After a while, Williams was so good at running with the ball that Moss and his friends would joke that they were going to beat him up if he did not start throwing him some touchdowns.

Williams literally grew up at Dupont. His father was a state trooper who was stationed at the school. Williams, his father, and his brother all lived in a trailer at the back of the school property. While this cut down on his commute to school, it also had another huge advantage.

Williams' father had the keys to the school, which allowed him to get into the gym whenever he wanted. This allowed him to practice his basketball skills, which would one day send him to the NBA.

It's nearly impossible to believe that a high school the size of Dupont could produce four future professional athletes. Two NFL players, Moss and Howard, an NBA world champion, Williams, and a baseball player, Singleton. There must have been something in the water.

During Williams' senior season and Moss's junior year, the two future pros would put on a show for the locals. They led Dupont to the state championship game and both were named Co-Players of the Year in the state of West Virginia.

"People would drive from miles away to see them play," Dupont basketball coach Jim Fout said. "We'd pull them away from ESPN and TNT. The kids were better entertainers."[vi]

By his senior season, Moss was already a West Virginia legend, but what he did not know was that he would be entering into the most rewarding, frustrating, happy, depressed, and tumultuous time of his young life.

Being on the field was the easy part for Moss. He dominated yet again as a senior, putting up 39 receptions for 808 yards and 14 touchdowns. He was named the West Virginia Player of the Year for the second straight season. He was also a Parade All-American for the first time.[vii]

"We'd be so far ahead in games," Singleton Jr. said. "We'd be signing autographs at halftime. And not just kids. Adults, moms, everyone."[viii]

That kind of celebrity for an African American athlete at Dupont did not go unnoticed by the white population at the school, especially when college coaches started showing up to recruit Moss and his friends.

There was a section of lockers at the school that was dubbed "Redneck Alley" by the African American students. Kids decorated their lockers in that area with Confederate flags and Ku Klux Klan symbols. Moss and his friends were victims of frequent taunts and racial slurs coming from Redneck Alley, but for the most part, Moss tried to ignore them.

When Moss and Williams were winning basketball games for Dupont, even Williams was at the receiving end of those racial slurs, despite the fact that he was white. He would stand up for his friend and teammate but would be ridiculed by the other white students.

"There are a lot of things about West Virginia you can't possibly understand unless you are from there," Williams said. "I tried to explain, 'He's a person, just like me.' But they didn't want to hear that."[ix]

Despite the negative attention from the other students, Moss was getting a ton of positive attention from college coaches. By rule, the NCAA allows a student-athlete to take five official visits, but Moss's mother only allowed him to take three. He chose to go to Florida, Tennessee, and Notre Dame.

With his three choices of schools, Moss faced even more scrutiny from the students and adults back at Dupont. Many resented the fact that Moss chose to not even visit West Virginia University. The students in "Redneck Alley" added that to the list of their perceived grievances against Moss and continually harassed him as a result.

Moss had his choice of schools, but in his mind, there was only one that would be the right fit for him: Notre Dame. The Fighting Irish had an advantage over all other schools at that time. This was before you could watch every available game in the world on ESPN Plus or online. Notre Dame was the only university at the time that had its own television contract and was seen nationwide on NBC every Saturday.

"With Notre Dame playing every Saturday with those gold helmets," Moss said. "I just fell in love with Notre Dame."[x]

And Notre Dame fell in love with Moss, or at least Irish Head Coach Lou Holtz did.

"The day I went to his house for my visit, there were only two soft chairs in the living room," Holtz said. "I sat in one, and Randy's mom sat in the other. Randy sat on the arm, right next to his mother. Throughout the recruiting process, he showed her the utmost respect. I'll never forget that."[xi]

Moss would ultimately sign his letter of intent to play football for the Notre Dame Fighting Irish, but he would not be going alone. His friend and lifelong teammate Bobby Howard also signed with Notre Dame to play linebacker. The two friends who played every sport together as kids would be headed to South Bend, Indiana, to continue their journey together, or so it would seem.

As football season turned into basketball season, the world of Randy Moss started to shift again. Moss dated Libby Offutt, who was white, throughout high school, and during their senior year, she gave birth to a daughter, Sydney. The racial slurs and epitaphs from "Redneck Alley" were relentless toward Moss and Offutt's relationship and daughter, but for the time being, Moss continued his work on the court and tried to ignore it.

The basketball season would help to show that Moss may be the greatest athlete ever to come out of the state of West Virginia. He averaged more than 30 points and 13 rebounds a game and for the second straight season was named the West Virginia High School Basketball Player of the Year. This time he did not have to share the honor with Williams. He was also a *USA Today* Honorable Mention All-American.[xii]

Moss's high school accomplishments were otherworldly. He won two state championships in football and was twice named West Virginia High School Player of the Year and he was an All-American. On the basketball court, he was Dupont's all-time leading scorer with more than 1,700 career points. He was also twice named the West Virginia Player of the Year, a feat that not even the best basketball player to ever come out of the state, Jerry West, ever accomplished.

In the springtime, Moss headed to the baseball field and the track. In his one season participating in track, he won the 100- and 200-meter state titles. He also led the baseball team to the state championship game.

As his accomplishments grew, Moss became more of a celebrity in town and in the state, something his mother tried desperately to protect him from.

"I couldn't shield him enough," Maxine Moss said. "You couldn't turn on the TV or open the newspaper without seeing him there. We're talking about a high school sophomore getting interviewed, and I never thought that was needed. But the more I didn't want it, the more it would come."[xiii]

But as his celebrity increased, Moss was more drawn into himself. He is, by nature, an introvert, despite all outward appearances to the contrary. During his senior year, Moss would frequently disappear from class. His teachers thought he was just going to the bathroom, but his disappearances started lasting longer and longer.

Eventually, a curious teacher followed Moss to find out what he had been doing. The results of his search astounded him. Moss would sneak away from class to play with Ronald, a boy with Down Syndrome. Ronald had no idea that Moss was a sports hero and in turn, Ronald had no expectations of Moss. They were just friends.

"Randy was so great with that boy," Dupont basketball coach Jim Fout said. "You wish other people saw that side of him."[xiv]

Despite his tenderness with Ronald, Moss was still subject to ridicule from "Redneck Alley." And during his senior year, it finally came to a head.

One afternoon, Moss's friend, Rayshawn Smith, came to find him. Someone had written a racial slur on Smith's desk. Smith implored Moss to watch his back as he challenged Ernest Ray Johnson to a fight. Smith believed that it was Johnson who had written the slur on his desk.

The two fought and Johnson was on the floor when Moss got involved. He kicked Johnson, leaving him with internal injuries that required a hospital stay.

"In a fight, you don't think," Moss said. "It was just my temper took over—like I was another person."[xv]

In most cases, school fights are handled by the school, but this was different. There was the racial aspect, with the majority white community of Belle looking for revenge. And then there was the Moss aspect. He was a celebrity and heading to Notre Dame. But he had also disrespected West Virginia University and there was also resentment over that.

The prosecutor in the case charged Moss as an adult with malicious wounding, which is a felony in West Virginia. Moss was expelled from school and forced to attend Cabell Alternative School for the remainder of the year.

"Basically, I had a lot of anger built up in me," Moss said. "The problems with me getting in trouble were me trying to express what I was going through at that time."[xvi]

Eventually, Moss pleaded guilty to two counts of misdemeanor battery and was sentenced to 30 days in prison. He was allowed to delay his prison sentence until after his freshman year at college. At the hearing, Moss apologized to Johnson and his family, but by then, it was too late.[xvii]

"It was a bad scene," Fout said. "What Randy did was wrong. He knows that. But if it had been just another student in the school and not Randy Moss, it never would have become what it did. The student would have been disciplined, for sure, but that prosecuting attorney, once he heard it was Moss, he was going after him."[xviii]

When Notre Dame heard about the fight and the conviction, they revoked his admission, despite the pleas from Holtz. Just like that, it was seemingly all gone for Moss and it appeared as though he was just going to be another alumnus of "Rand University."

"A lot of us don't dream past high school," Singleton Jr. said. "That's the end for a lot of us. For all the has-beens, Rand University is there. That's your college. That's where you're going."[xix]

But, as it turned out, all was not lost for Moss. After Notre Dame rescinded his admission, Holtz made a call down to Florida State to discuss the situation with his friend Bobby Bowden. Bowden was a legend at Florida State and could get Moss into the university if he chose to. Furthermore, the Seminoles were coming off a 10-1-1 season and could always use more talent.

Florida State agreed to accept Moss as a student under two conditions: he would have to sit out his first season with the team and he could not get into any further trouble.

For now, Moss would be headed to Tallahassee as an observer of the 1995 Florida State football team, but he would almost immediately show that he belonged.

Chapter 2: College Career

Florida State

In the 1990s, Florida State was the most dominant college football program in the nation. The Seminoles won two national championships and were never ranked lower than fourth in the AP postseason poll throughout the entire decade. They have produced dozens of future NFL players, but when it comes to pure athletes, Deion Sanders is the one that they are all measured against. Sanders played football, baseball, and also ran track at the school. He would eventually go on to a Hall-of-Fame career as a cornerback in the NFL, but also played Major League Baseball.

When Sanders was on campus with the Seminoles, he ran the fastest 40-yard dash in school history at 4.21 seconds. It was one of the best times ever run by any human being. When Moss arrived on campus, he was timed at 4.25 seconds, the second-fastest in school history.

Florida State was the number-one team in the polls coming into the 1995 season, even without Moss on the field. In the first seven games of the season, the Seminole's offense put up a whopping 393 points, a 56-points-per-game average.

It was their defense, though, that was one of the best units in the country. Through the first seven games, the defense was only giving up 17 points a game, and the vast majority of those points came long after the starters had left the field in blowouts.

The toughest challenge for the Florida State defense did not come on Saturdays, but during the week in practice. It was there that they faced the best receiver in the country: Randy Moss. He routinely torched one of the best defenses in the country, but it was only in practice. So, no one got to see how truly great Moss was. Yet.

The Seminoles ended the 1995 season at 10-2, winning the Orange Bowl over Moss's other team, Notre Dame.

Moss stayed out of trouble for his freshman year, but he still had to return to West Virginia to serve his 30-day prison sentence.

When Moss returned to complete his sentence, he was drug-tested as a part of his intake. Unfortunately, he tested positive for marijuana. Thus, he had broken the terms of his plea deal and was immediately sent to prison for an as-yet-to-be-determined amount of time.

News reached Florida State of his positive test and Moss was immediately expelled from the university and kicked off the football team.

"It broke my heart because I couldn't give him a second chance," Bowden said. "I want to save my boys if I can because if I can't, they're back out on the street, and I don't want them back out there on the street."[xx]

Within one year, Moss had been kicked out of two colleges and lost two Division I scholarships. It appeared that Rand University was going to get him too.

Moss spent the first seven days of his prison sentence in solitary confinement. When Moss was brought before the judge after the seven days, he told him that he wanted to be better and wanted another chance at life. The judge sent Moss back to prison to await sentencing.

In the two years prior to Moss's case, not a single person in the state of West Virginia had had their probation revoked because of a positive marijuana test. Moss's lawyer, Tim DiPiero, knew that there was more at work in this case. The state was still bitter over Moss leaving and not giving West Virginia University the respect they felt it deserved and now they were using their opportunity to get revenge.

DiPiero enlisted the help of a minister from Charleston to help galvanize the African American community in West Virginia. Reverend Matthew Watts was a powerful voice within the state and DiPiero was able to convince him to help Moss. But both men knew that this was going to be an uphill battle.

"You have to understand what was happening in the 90s," Watts said. "This was on the heels of the OJ case. There was a lot of hate and animus toward pampered black athletes. Randy made a tragic misstep in his career with how he treated West Virginia. He didn't even take a visit to the school. A lot of people were furious."[xxi]

With Watts in his corner, Moss appeared before a judge and asked for a second chance. It seemed the judge was leaning toward giving Moss another 90 days in prison, on top of the time that he had already served, but it was Watts' plea that helped spare Moss.

"We don't throw young people away because they commit youthful acts of indiscretion," Watts said at the trial.[xxii] "We don't ruin their lives. We don't ruin their careers. We still believe in him (Moss)."

The judge agreed with Watts' assessment of Moss and reduced his sentence to 60 days, including time served. This would allow Moss to be out of prison in time for the 1996 college football season.

But there was still one problem. He did not have a team.

Marshall

Most people have no idea where Marshall University is located. The university is in Huntington, West Virginia, just over the state border from Ohio. In the 1960s, their football program was the butt of several jokes. Its home stadium was in such deplorable shape that it was condemned. And on top of that, the beleaguered school was hit with more than 100 recruiting violations.

Eventually, the football program was thrown out of the Mid-American Conference and forced into the nomad land of college football: independent teams. And then the most tragic event in the history of college football occurred.

The Marshall football team was coming home from a loss to East Carolina when the team's plane crashed, killing everyone on board, including 37 players, the coaches, team doctors, the athletic director, and 25 boosters.[xxiii]

Eventually, the football team would recover, but it would take years. Coach Jim Donnan took over the program in 1990 and led Marshall to the 1992 Division 1AA National Title. Marshall was in the process of returning to Division when Donnan left to take over at Georgia in 1995.

In 1996, Marshall hired former Florida defensive coordinator and alumnus Bob Pruett to take over the team. In a perfect coincidence for Moss, it turned out that Pruett was the man who had actually recruited him at the University of Florida. With both Moss and

Pruett being from West Virginia, there was a natural connection between the two of them.

There was also an advantage that Marshall had over every other school that was looking at Moss. Because Marshall was still a Division 1AA school, Randy could transfer and be eligible to play immediately. If he had decided to transfer to any other Division 1 school, he would have had to sit out another season.

With few other options and his familiarity with Pruett, Moss decided to enroll at Marshall for the 1996 season.

"This was a natural fit for Randy," Pruett said. "He could transfer down and not have to sit out. And he could still get into Division 1 football and get a chance to play WVU (in 1997). It was just a win-win. The cards fell good. It was a good deal for all of us."[xxiv]

Moss was not just heading to any team; he was heading to one of the best Division 1AA programs. Not only had the Thundering Herd won the national title in 1992 but it had also played in the championship game three other times in the 1990s. It also had capable quarterbacks waiting for him in future NFL star Chad Pennington and Florida transfer Eric Kresser.

When Moss arrived on campus, he was already a West Virginia celebrity, but now people expected the world of him.

"The legend of Randy Moss had already existed, but to know he was coming to Marshall to play... it kind of just set up for him," Marshall play-by-play announcer Keith Morehouse said. "But it didn't really hit you until you saw him in practice. Then you realized what kind of talent he was."[xxv]

But Moss had changed over the past two years because of his experiences. After the fight, his time in prison, and losing two football scholarships, he became more withdrawn and did not trust many people.

"You've got to put yourself in that person's shoes and realize and understand how he's able to do what he's doing," Moss's best friend Tyrone Carter said. "At a young age, he was accused of doing something he didn't do and was put behind bars. That's tough, man. It continues to have an effect on your life. He trusted people who hurt him, and it took time for him to trust people again. And I grew up in the same kind of setting he did, so I can relate a lot."[xxvi]

But one thing about Moss did not change. After two years of not playing football, Moss stepped back on the field and absolutely dominated. Marshall finished the regular season at 11-0, with the offense averaging 42 points a game and winning every game by at least two touchdowns.

Moss attacked the Division 1AA record books. He tied Jerry Rice's single-season touchdown record with 28. He set a record for most receiving yards by a freshman with 1,709, a record that still stands today. He also set the record for most games with a touchdown (11) and most consecutive games with a touchdown (13). He also returned kickoffs for the Thundering Herd, averaging 34 yards a return.[xxvii]

"It was astonishing how good he was each Saturday," Morehouse said. "He just did things that were otherworldly as opposed to what I'd seen anyone in football do, personally."[xxviii]

Despite their overwhelming season, Marshall entered the 1AA Football Tournament as the number-two seed, behind once-beaten Montana. The Thundering Herd opened the playoffs against the University of Delaware's Fightin' Blue Hens. Moss set the 1AA Playoff record for receiving yards with 288 in a 59-14 win.

After also blowing out Furman and Northern Iowa, Moss and Marshall took on top-seeded Montana. The Grizzlies had beaten Marshall the previous season in the 1AA Championship game—but that was without Moss. In the game, Moss exploded against Montana. He set a 1AA Playoff record with four touchdown receptions in one game. He caught nine passes for 220 yards in Marshall's 49-29 win.[xxix]

The game was held at Marshall's home field, so the stadium erupted. While the entire university celebrated a national championship, Moss, the hero of the game, quietly went back to his room and went to sleep.

"I really wasn't caught up in that hype," Moss said. "I couldn't tell you how crazy the campus was. Just for the fact that I was stabbed in the back so many times trying to do what I loved, which was football. My mental just wasn't right."[xxx]

Despite all that, Moss would set the Division 1AA record for most touchdown catches in a playoff tournament with 9, and most yards in a tournament with 636.

Marshall would be heading to Division 1A for the 1997 season and Moss had some extra motivation. The Herd's first game of the season and its first game in D1A would be against West Virginia. It would be

Moss's chance to show the entire state just how good he was.

"My whole focus all offseason was to go up there and tear West Virginia's head completely off," Moss said.[xxxi]

In the game, Moss caught 7 passes for 85 yards and 2 touchdowns, including a score that put Marshall up by 3 late in the fourth quarter against the 13th-ranked Mountaineers. But it would be Pennington that undid the Herd on that day. He threw four interceptions, including two costly picks in the fourth quarter that led to a West Virginia 42-31 victory. Nevertheless, Moss had proven his point to the state, and he had much more to show.

The next week against Army, Moss caught 5 passes for 186 yards and 2 touchdowns, including a career-long 90-yard touchdown catch. Moss dominated the game, outjumping, outrunning, and running over defenders. It was one of the best performances that West Point had ever seen.

It seemed like every week, Moss was doing something spectacular. Against Ball State, he set the school record by catching five touchdown passes. He was the new human highlight reel.

"For us as quarterbacks, we just had to put it (the football) in the area," Pennington said. "We didn't even have to be that accurate."[xxxii]

Despite his accomplishments on the field, Moss still kept to himself off the field. There was always that overriding sense within him that the people of West Virginia were out to get him and if he happened to slip up one more time, it would all be over. And he also knew that there was a future for him.

"One more screw-up, and I've got nothing else to look for in life," Moss said. "So, if staying at home, watching TV, and playing at my PlayStation are going to keep me out of trouble, even if I'm bored, I can do it for a couple of months. It's all about that money, man.

That money is clanging. If you get the opportunity, you got to go get it."[xxxiii]

Marshall finished the regular season at 9-2 and won a spot in the MAC Championship game against Toledo. In the third quarter, Marshall was clinging to a 10-7 lead when Pennington hit Moss for a 75-yard touchdown pass, putting the Herd in front 17-7 and essentially putting the game away. Marshall would go on to win the inaugural MAC Championship game 34-14.

The victory earned Marshall a trip to the Motor City Bowl in Detroit to take on Ole Miss. With the Herd down 7-0, Pennington hit Moss for an 80-yard touchdown reception on the first offensive play from scrimmage for Marshall, tying the score. It would be Moss's 54th career touchdown catch. He would score at least one touchdown in all 28 games that he played at Marshall.[xxxiv]

The game went back and forth until Mississippi's Deuce McAllister scored from one yard out with 31 seconds remaining to give Ole Miss a 34-31 lead. On the game's final play, Pennington hit Moss for a 40-yard reception. As he was trying to pitch the ball to a teammate to continue the game, the ball was fumbled and Mississippi recovered, ending the game. It would be Moss's final play with the Herd.

Moss ended his second season with Marshall with 96 receptions for 1,820 yards and 26 touchdowns. He received the Fred Biletnikoff Award as the Nation's top receiver and he was invited to New York as a finalist for the Heisman Trophy.

The 1997 Heisman Trophy ceremony may have been one of the most talented rosters ever. It featured three future Hall-of-Famers and Ryan Leaf. Charles Woodson of Michigan won the award, becoming the first defensive player to ever win it. He just barely beat out Tennessee's Peyton Manning.

Throughout the ceremony, Moss wore dark sunglasses, even though it took place indoors and at night. He later revealed that he wore them because he was so nervous, he was scared to have anyone look him in the eyes.

In two seasons at Marshall, Moss had shown the world what he was capable of on the field, but was it enough for everyone to forget what he had done off the field? Moss was now headed to the NFL draft to find out.

NFL Draft

Since 1980, only two receivers were taken with the first overall pick in the draft. Irving Fryar was selected first by the New England Patriots in 1984 out of Nebraska, and the Jets selected Keyshawn Johnson out of USC in 1996. In his final season with the Trojans, Johnson caught 102 passes for 1,434 yards and only 7 touchdowns.

In comparison, Moss's Marshall numbers dwarfed Keyshawn's. Moss had 26 touchdowns and 1,820 yards. It was clear, based on talent alone, that Moss should have been at least a top-five pick.

But the draft is not necessarily based solely on talent. Teams were already steering away from Moss because of his earlier off-the-field issues. Yes, they were enamored with his talent, but there was everything else to consider.

It then did not help that Moss skipped the NFL Combine. At first, he did not offer an explanation, which allowed rumors to spread that he skipped it in order to avoid the drug test. But after a few days, Moss's agent revealed that Moss had had six teeth extracted and was forced to miss the combine as a result. Still, the damage was done.[xxxv]

Moss performed for scouts at Marshall's Pro Day, running a 4.25 40-yard dash. Every NFL team sent a scout, but none were more impressed than the Dallas Cowboys. Dallas owned the eighth pick and assumed that Moss would drop to them. They led Moss to believe that if he was still available, Dallas would select him.

On draft day, Moss gathered with some friends and family members at his mother's home in Rand and waited for his name to be called. The first two picks were virtually assured: Peyton Manning and Ryan Leaf.

As the first seven picks passed, Moss was still on the board. When the commissioner reached the podium for Dallas' pick, it wasn't Randy Moss's name that was called. The Cowboys selected defensive end Greg Ellis out of North Carolina.

"I'm looking at my momma," Moss said. "Now, she don't care nothing about sports. She's got the Bible on her lap and she's ready to celebrate with me. She was more hurt than I was."[xxxvi]

The draft continued and Moss's name still was not being called. He was not even the first wide receiver selected. That honor went to Kevin Dyson out of Utah, who Tennessee took at 17.

Finally, as the draft went into the 20s, Moss got a phone call from Dennis Green, head coach of the Minnesota Vikings.

"The guy could really run and make plays," Green said. "We were convinced, a lot of people weren't, but we were convinced his off-the-field incidents when he was younger were part of being young, but his love of the game would keep him from committing the same type of mistakes later, because if you make those mistakes, you can't play, and Randy really wanted to play, and we were right about that. He loved to play the game and play the game with a lot of enthusiasm, and it's why he went on to be so successful because his behavior was a thing of the past and he was all about the future."xxxvii

Greene was right about Moss. He would end up being one of the four future Hall-of-Famers that were selected in that first round. He had to wait, but eventually, Moss got his team and his day.

With the 21st pick in the 1998 NFL Draft, the Minnesota Vikings selected Randy Moss out of Marshall University.

Chapter 3: Pro Career

New Start in Minnesota

The Minnesota Vikings have a long and storied history of futility. They are one of only two teams in NFL history to go to four Super Bowls and lose all four. It seems the team is just good enough to tease their fans into believing, only to tear the rug out from under them in the playoffs.

The team that Randy Moss went to, though, was very close to being great. Rob Johnson and Randall Cunningham were the two quarterbacks, and the wide receiver room had Jake Reed and future Hall-of-Famer Cris Carter. Carter took Moss under his wing and tried to mentor him and teach him the ways of NFL life. But Moss being Moss, some of those lessons did not easily take.

The Vikings were coming off a good season. They had lost in the Divisional Round of the playoffs to the

49ers. There was nothing that could have prepared them for what was about to happen in 1998.

Minnesota's Week 1 game was against the Tampa Bay Buccaneers. Tampa was coming off a 10-6 record and the team's first playoff appearance since 1982. Many of the pieces that would win the team the Super Bowl a few years later were already in place, including Warren Sapp, Derrick Brooks, John Lynch, and Ronde Barber.

But with Carter and Reed already on the field, the Bucs were going to have to enlist the services of second-year cornerback Floyd Young against Moss. Coming into the game, Young had confidence in the game plan.

"We're anticipating them to come out in three-wide receiver sets," Young said. "Because of the addition of Randy Moss, you can't afford to keep a player like that off the field. They'll try to make it a wide-open game. They'll try to make it a track meet. But we have confidence that our coaching staff is going to put us in the right position to make plays."[xxxviii]

Young's confidence was misplaced.

In his first career game, Randy Moss announced his presence to the rest of the league and the world in general. He caught touchdown passes of 48 and 31 yards in the first half and ended the game with four catches for 95 yards. Minnesota would win the game 31-7.

Thus, the Minnesota offense was off and running. In the first seven games of the season, they averaged 35 points a game and won all seven games. Moss was in the process of having one of the greatest rookie seasons for a receiver in the history of the NFL.

The Vikings were 10-1 heading into Dallas for a Thanksgiving Day game. Moss grew up a Cowboys fan, but Dallas had passed on him in the draft after telling him they would select him. It was time for Moss to get his revenge.

On the game's fourth play, Cunningham hit Moss on a 51-yard touchdown bomb. In the second quarter, Cunningham again connected with Moss, this time on a 56-yard touchdown. It was his second catch of the game and his second touchdown.

In the third quarter, Cunningham threw a four-yard completion to Moss. He broke a tackle and took off down the sideline. At the Dallas 10-yard line, Cowboy's defensive back Terry Billups had an angle to take him down. But Moss came to a complete stop, and Billups ran right past him and off the field. Moss walked into the end zone for this third touchdown of the game and made Billups look silly in the process.[xxxix]

Moss finished the 46-36 victory with three catches for 163 yards and 3 touchdowns. After the game, he left the locker room without speaking to the media, instead letting his play do the talking.

Minnesota finished the regular season at 15-1. The Vikings' offense set a new NFL record by scoring 556 points. They were only the third team in NFL history to win 15 games in the regular season.

Moss finished his rookie year with 69 catches for 1,313 yards and a rookie-record 17 touchdowns. He was the Offensive Rookie of the Year and came in third in the MVP voting. He was also First-Team All-Pro and made the Pro Bowl.[xl]

The Vikings were the top seed in the NFC and got a first-round bye. In the Divisional Round, they easily dispatched the Arizona Cardinals, 41-21, setting up an NFC Championship game against Atlanta.

The Falcons were the second-best team in the NFC with a 14-2 record, but with their high-flying offense, Minnesota was a heavy favorite in the game. Down 7-0 in the first quarter, Cunningham connected with Moss for a 31-yard touchdown to tie the score.

In the second quarter, the Vikings were up 20-7 with the ball on Atlanta's 18-yard line. Another touchdown could have broken Atlanta's back, but Cunningham was sacked and fumbled the ball. Atlanta recovered and scored on the ensuing drive to cut Minnesota's halftime lead to 20-14.

Minnesota had a 27-20 lead with a little more than two minutes remaining in the game. Vikings' kicker Gary Anderson came out to attempt a 38-yard field goal to essentially seal the game. At the time, Anderson had the best statistical season of any kicker in NFL history, going 35-for-35 on field goal attempts. But his kick sailed wide left, giving Atlanta hope.

The Falcons were able to march down the field to tie the score at 27, sending the game into overtime. In overtime, the teams exchanged punts, but on their second possession, Atlanta drove the ball down the field. Atlanta's Morten Andersen kicked a 39-yard field goal to win the game and send the Falcons to their first-ever Super Bowl.[xli]

Atlanta would go on to get crushed in the Super Bowl by the Denver Broncos in John Elway's final game.

The Vikings, meanwhile, were left to pick up the pieces after another heartbreaking loss.

"It would've changed the legacy of everybody involved with that team," Vikings' vice-president Jeff Diamond said years later. "Everybody who played, and Dennis Green as a coach. It was disappointing the way we lost. And there's no guarantee that we would've beaten the Broncos, but it would've been nice to get there. It would've been a great accomplishment in and of itself."[xlii]

In 2023, *USA Today* named the 1998 Vikings as the best team to never make it to a Super Bowl and the second-best team not to win a Super Bowl, behind another Moss team, the 2007 Patriots.[xliii]

At the start of the 1999 season, it was clear that there was a hangover for Moss and the entire team. The Vikings started out 2-4 and Moss only had 4 touchdown receptions and 31 overall catches. In response to the team's downward slide, Green benched starting quarterback Cunningham in favor of former first-overall pick Jeff George.

With George at the helm, the Vikings finished the season 8-2. Moss's numbers even started to pick up with the strong-armed George throwing him bombs. In a Week 10 game against the Bears, Moss caught a career-high 12 passes for a career-high 204 yards.

A 10-6 record was good enough to get the Vikings into the playoffs as a wild card. They would host Moss's nemesis, the Dallas Cowboys. The Cowboys had been the best team in the 1990s, but before they could play the playoff game at Minnesota, the decade ended. This game would be the last time that three legendary Cowboys offensive stars, Troy Aikman, Emmitt Smith, and Michael Irvin, would ever play together.

The Cowboys jumped out to a 17-0 lead. Late in the second quarter, George hit Moss for a four-yard touchdown pass to cut into the Cowboys' lead. Just before the half, Smith would get his hand caught in a

Vikings' defensive player's helmet, breaking his hand. He would not return to the game.

Losing Smith proved to be the difference in the second half. The Cowboys had no running game, and the Vikings' defense could tee-off on Aikman. The Vikings outscored the Cowboys 20-0 in the second half, taking the game 27-17. Moss caught 5 passes for 127 yards and a touchdown.

The Vikings next headed to St. Louis to take on the Greatest Show on Turf. The Rams had discovered the untapped greatness of backup quarterback Kurt Warner and were putting up points in bunches. Warner and St. Louis surprised the entire league as they won the NFC West and were the top seed in the NFC.

The Vikings' defense stepped up in the first half and held the Rams' offense to only 14 points, and Minnesota was holding on to a 17-14 lead. It looked like the Vikings were going to be able to end the

Warner fairy tale, but then the second half kickoff ended that hope.

The Rams returner Tony Horne took the second-half kickoff 95 yards for a touchdown. The kickoff return sparked a 35-0 run by the Rams over a quarter and a half. When the Rams had finished, the Vikings' season was over, 49-37. Moss caught 9 passes for 188 yards and 2 touchdowns, but it just was not enough.[xliv]

During the game, Moss was caught squirting an official with a water bottle out of frustration. In the moment, Moss was upset that the official had missed a critical interference call that could have made a significant difference in the game. But of course, you simply cannot disrespect a referee no matter how questionable the call, or *non-call*, as the case may be. Unsurprisingly, the NFL did not take too kindly to his gesture. Moss was fined $40,000, but it was later reduced to $25,000 with the understanding that if it happened again, Moss was going to get another fine. It was the first of what would be many minor run-ins with officials and the league.

After the Vikings' season ended, Moss headed to the Pro Bowl again. This time he lit up the screen. He had 9 catches for 212 yards and a touchdown. He was named the game's MVP.

The 2000 season brought about big changes in Minnesota. Gone were veteran quarterbacks Cunningham and George. In their place was second-year quarterback Dante Culpepper. The Vikings used their first-round pick in 1999 on Culpepper, and now was his time to take over the reins.

The youngster did not disappoint. Minnesota started the season 7-0, and Moss was averaging a touchdown a game. It appeared the Vikings' magic was back. After two straight losses, the Vikings won another four in a row, but the biggest game was again on Thanksgiving.

For the second time in three seasons, the Vikings headed to Dallas to take on the Vikings for Thanksgiving. Moss ended the game with 7 catches for 144 yards and 2 touchdowns. One of his touchdowns was positively inhuman. Moss jumped in the air for the ball with nearly his entire body out-of-bounds and somehow came down with his toes inbounds for the score.

For the third time since the Cowboys failed to draft him, Moss and the Vikings beat the Cowboys. In those three games, Moss had 15 catches for 434 yards and 6 touchdowns.

The Vikings finished the regular season at 11-5. They won the NFC Central and received a first-round bye. In the Divisional Round, the Vikings hosted the New Orleans Saints. On the third play of the game, Culpepper hit Moss for a 53-yard touchdown, and the rout was on. Minnesota went on to win the game 34-16.

Moss only caught 2 passes but they were for 121 yards and 2 touchdowns.

For the second time in three years, the Vikings were back in the NFC Championship game. This time they headed to New Jersey to take on the Giants, the top overall seed in the NFC.

The Giants won the coin toss and took the opening kickoff 74 yards right down the Vikings' throat. Then, on the ensuing kickoff, the Vikings fumbled the ball. The Giants recovered and quickly scored another touchdown. Just like that, it was 14-0, and the game was basically over.

By halftime, the Giants were up 34-0, a record for the largest deficit in an NFC Championship game. The Vikings' offense simply never got started. Moss only caught 2 passes for 18 yards in the entire game. The Giants won 41-0 and were headed to the Super Bowl.

"I don't think I've ever been in a game like that," Giants Coach Jim Fassel said. "We just annihilated them. It wasn't luck, it wasn't like at the last minute. We just kicked their butt right from the beginning."[xlv]

After three seasons in the NFL, Randy Moss had become the only player to have more than 4,000 yards receiving and 40 touchdowns, but what alluded him was a trip to the Super Bowl.

The Wilderness

Minnesota had the window wide open for them, but it appeared as though it was closing quickly. Longtime defensive tackle John Randle left the team in the offseason, and despite leading the team to two NFC Championship games, coach Dennis Green appeared to be on the hot seat.

The team seemed stressed when it opened training camp after losing the NFC Championship game to the Giants, and then tragedy struck. The team's best offensive lineman, Korey Stringer, passed out during training camp practice and later died of heat stroke.

With the team dealing with so much adversity, it was easy to see why their minds may not necessarily be on football.

Moss, though, was looking for something for himself. He was heading into the final season of his rookie contract and was only scheduled to make $3.5 million. Moss and his agent, Dante DiTrapano, were looking for him to not just be the highest-paid receiver, but the highest-paid player in the league.

Eventually, Moss and the Vikings agreed to an eight-year, $75-million contract, which included a $10-million signing bonus. The contract would make Moss the highest-paid non-quarterback in the league.

"It was important for him to be recognized not only as the best wide receiver in the game, but as one of the best players in the league," said DiTrapano.[xlvi]

Despite the contract extension, the 2001 season was a disaster for the Vikings. The team started the year 3-3 but then went 2-8 for the remainder of the season.

Moss had 1,233 yards on 82 catches and 10 touchdowns but did not make the Pro Bowl for the first time in his career.[xlvii]

Just prior to the team's final game against Baltimore, rumors began to spread that Green was going to be fired after the season. After a meeting with the team's owner, Red McCombs, Green was let go just before the final game of the season. Assistant head coach Mike Tice would coach the team's final game.

Green had spent 10 seasons in Minnesota, and 2001 was his only losing season. He was also only the second African American head coach in the history of the NFL after Art Shell, who was hired by the Raiders.

"Some guys who most people never thought would have played in the National Football League, but they were looking for an opportunity," Green said. "Those are the type of players that made up the 10 years that we've been here with the Minnesota Vikings. What we try to do is treat them all the same. We try to give them all an opportunity to reach their goals to reach their dreams to be successful. And that's something I've enjoyed."

One of those players was Randy Moss. Green was mostly responsible for the Vikings taking a chance on him in the draft, and that chance mostly paid off for Minnesota.

"I really don't know why I was treated the way I was treated on draft day," Moss said after Green passed away in 2016. "But Coach Green gave me an opportunity, and I told him, 'Coach, you're not going to regret this.' The man passed away without me really, really, really giving him my love and thanks for what he was able to do for me and my family. There's a lot of teams out there that passed on me for wrong reasons. Coach Green gave me that opportunity."[xlviii]

To replace Green, the Vikings decided that Tice would remain as the head coach for the 2002 season. Tice came to a realization that his greatest asset was Moss, and it was imperative that he got the ball as often as possible.

To that end, Tice created the "Randy Rules." Essentially, the goal was to get Moss the ball as much as possible, and to do that, Moss was going to run shorter routes and have the opportunity to run after the catch. In the 2001 season, when Moss was targeted more than 40% of the time, the team was 5-1, but they were 0-10 when he was targeted less than 40% of the time.

Most people were surprised when Tice mentioned the "Randy Rules" in public. It was like telling the other teams what you were going to do before you actually did it. And in the NFL, there are typically dire consequences when you tip your hand. By Week 6, the Vikings were 1-5. Moss only had 40 receptions and 2 touchdowns. The "Randy Rules" were abandoned, and the team went back to its normal offense.

"I didn't really care much about the Randy Ratio when it was brought up," Moss said. "I just wanted to win."[xlix]

After a Week 3 loss to the Carolina Panthers, Moss found himself back in trouble with the law because of a traffic violation. He was trying to make an illegal turn down a street in Minneapolis when a traffic officer suddenly stepped in front of his car and fell to the ground, sustaining a slight injury.

Moss, who seemed to have an uncanny ability to attract bad luck and publicity, was arrested as a result of the incident and originally charged with second-degree assault, a felony in the state of Minnesota. He was released on bail and continued playing the season with the Vikings. Moss would later plead guilty to two traffic violations, which resulted in 30 days spent in prison and a $1,200 fine.[l]

It would be another lost season in Minnesota. The team ended the year at 6-10. Although Moss had a career-high 106 catches, only 7 of them were for touchdowns, a career-low.[li]

By the 2003 season, Moss was entering his sixth year in the league. Even though he was only 26 at the time, he became one of the leaders of the Vikings. Moss had lost both of his mentors in Coach Green and fellow receiver Cris Carter, who had left the team after the 2001 season. It was now Moss's turn to take over the team.

It started in the offseason when Moss attended all of the Vikings' events. He even put on five pounds of muscle to improve his game.

"That just shows he is growing up," quarterback Dante Culpepper said. "Moss, he's just realizing he's a leader and he has to do it day-in and day-out. He leads by example, and he's understanding that more and more every day, and I'm glad to be playing with him."[lii]

The Vikings started the season 6-0 with Moss in his new leadership position. But after the hot start, the team lost its next four games. For the remainder of the year, the team would trade wins and losses, finally ending the year at 9-7. The Vikings' offense had the most yards in the NFL, but that did not translate into points, as the team was sixth in scoring.

The inconsistent play cost the Vikings the playoffs, as they lost the division to the Green Bay Packers by a game. A costly loss to Arizona then officially eliminated them from the playoffs.

Moss led the NFL with 17 touchdowns and set a new career-high with 111 receptions. He was named to the Pro Bowl for the fifth time in six seasons and First Team All-Pro for the third time in his career. But it was another lost season in Minnesota.[liii]

In his first six seasons in the NFL, Moss had not missed a single game due to injury. His consecutive start streak was over 100 heading into the 2004 season. But in a Week 5 win over the Saints, that streak was going to be in jeopardy.

In the second quarter of the game, Moss tripped over a Saints' defensive back and hurt his hamstring. He played the next series but then left the game and returned to the locker room.

Moss would play the following two weeks, mostly as a decoy, but after that, the pain was too much for him. He could not run routes, and in the two games he did play, he did not catch a single pass for the first time in his career.

After starting the season 4-1, the Vikings would be without Moss for three weeks. Including the two weeks he played sparingly, the Vikings went 2-3 without Moss at full strength. One of those games was a 34-31 loss to the Green Bay Packers at Lambeau Field. During the game, the Wisconsin band held up placards, spelling out "Where You At, Moss?" Moss would not forget that.

Moss was able to return for the final six games, but the Vikings' inconsistent play continued, with the team going 2-4 to finish the season at 8-8. Despite their record, the Vikings still managed to sneak into the playoffs as the sixth seed. Their Wild Card game would be again at Lambeau Field against the Packers.

Prior to the playoff game, Moss garnered some negative publicity yet again. In the team's season finale against Washington, Moss left the field prematurely with just two seconds remaining in the game and went to the locker room. After the game, Moss did not offer any explanation about his early exit, and most were not happy about what they perceived to be a display of disappointment.

"It shouldn't happen, and if it happens again there might be some problems," Vikings center Matt Birk said.[liv]

Even the Vikings' head coach had no answer for why Moss would leave the field.

"I understand his frustration," Tice said, "but we can't let our frustrations make us make poor decisions of poor judgment."[lv]

With inconsistent play and a poor record, it appeared as though the Vikings were set up for failure against the Packers, who had beaten them twice already that season.

But that is why they play the game. Seemingly before Green Bay even entered the field, the Vikings were up 17-0. Moss caught a first-quarter touchdown to make it 14-0, only five minutes into the game.

In the fourth quarter, the Packers scored to make it 24-17 with more than 13 minutes remaining in the game. And then Moss struck again. He caught a 34-yard pass from Culpepper to seal the victory. It was at that moment he did something else unexpected. He ran to the back of the end zone and pretended to moon the entire Packer crowd.

"Just having a little fun with the boys, a little bit," Moss said after the game. "I hope I don't get in trouble by it, but if I do, I'll take the heat."[lvi]

Moss's faux moon certainly took attention away from his walking off the field the previous week, but it also brought more negative attention to Moss. What had been nothing more than a playful gesture was harshly criticized and he was ultimately fined $10,000 by the NFL for the celebration.

The following week, the Vikings headed to Philly to take on the Eagles in the Divisional Round. Philadelphia was 13-3 and had long since locked up the top seed in the NFC. The Vikings were seemingly ill-prepared as they were blown out by the Eagles, 27-14. The team was incredibly sloppy, including a fake field-goal play when no receivers went out for a pass and the quarterback had no one to throw to.

"Mistakes, penalties at the wrong time, taking some points off the board, stopping a drive, having a nice play called back," said Tice, rattling off Minnesota's miscues. "We made some mistakes when we had a little bit of rhythm going. We didn't finish anything."[lvii]

Once again, Minnesota was headed home. In his career, Moss had played in eight playoff games with the Vikings. In those games, they had a 4-4 record, including two losses in the NFC Championship game. The loss to the Eagles would be the final playoff game of his Vikings career.

Lost in Oakland

A little over a month after their playoff loss, the Vikings started shopping Moss around to other teams. In late February, it was announced that Moss had been traded to the Oakland Raiders for two draft picks and linebacker Napoleon Harris.

"In speaking with Moss, although he has a lot of ties to Minnesota and did not particularly want to be traded, he's very excited with the possibility of playing for

Raiders owner Al Davis and being a part of the Raider tradition," Moss's Agent Dante DiTrapano said.[lviii]

Al Davis always had a soft spot in his heart for outlaws, especially outlaws that were incredibly fast. And it just so happened that Moss fit that bill. Despite the truth that much of the negative publicity that Moss attracted was largely unwarranted or exaggerated, he had become a scapegoat of sorts for the NFL and the media at large. Davis saw it as an opportunity for Moss to repair his image and lift the struggling Raiders franchise in the process.

The team that Moss was coming to, though, just was not any good. They were 5-11 the previous season and had just traded away their first draft pick to acquire Moss. The team had fading starts like Warren Sapp and Kerry Collins and a bunch of unproven young players.

The Raiders lost their first three games and final six games on their way to a 4-12 record. Moss had a career-low 60 receptions. After the season, Raiders coach Norv Turner was fired. In his place, Davis brought back former coach Art Shell. Shell was the first African American coach in the history of the NFL. He was also a Hall-of-Fame offensive lineman for the Raiders, making him royalty in Oakland.

But if possible, the situation in Oakland only got worse. The defense was solid, but the offense was terrible, averaging a little more than 10 points a game. The Raiders used three different quarterbacks throughout the season, and combined, they threw only seven touchdowns, three of which went to Moss. Moss had a career-low in receptions, yards, and touchdowns. Unsurprisingly, he was clearly not happy in Oakland, and he was perhaps a bit too vocal about that.

"Maybe because I'm unhappy, and I'm not too much excited about what's going on, so my concentration and focus level tends to go down when I'm in a bad mood," Moss said. "So, all I can say is if you put me in a good situation and make me happy, man, you get good results."[lix]

Moss missed the final three games of the season with an ankle injury. The Raiders ended the season at 2-14. In Moss's final game of the season, he had two catches for 28 yards. It would be his last game with the Raiders.

Redemption

After having acquired Moss for two draft picks and a player, new Raiders head coach Lane Kiffin decided to trade him to the New England Patriots for a fourth-round pick in the 2007 NFL Draft.

Of all the organizations in the NFL, New England may have been the best and only landing spot for Moss after his time in Oakland. His reputation, which had been plagued by some controversy to begin with, took even more hits while playing for the Raiders because of his lack of production.

But now he was headed to the premier organization in all of football. Going into the 2007 NFL Draft, the Patriots had already won three Super Bowls and were helmed by arguably the greatest coach of all time, Bill Belichick. The team also had a deep roster filled with veteran leaders, including GOAT quarterback Tom Brady.

In New England, Moss would not have to be the leader, nor would he be tasked with saving a team in deep chaos like Oakland, whose problems at the time frankly ran far deeper than any receiver position. He could just go out and play. He also did not have to carry the offense. That would be Brady's job.

"Just really last night me and coach Belichick really talked for the first time about what's been going on," Moss said. "He asked me how excited I would be if the opportunity would present itself for me to become a Patriot and, really, I was overwhelmed because I didn't expect to hear from coach Belichick. I've made a lot of money and I still have money in the bank. So, by me coming to an organization such as the New England Patriots, why would money be a factor? I'm still in awe that I'm a part of this organization."[lx]

Moss missed most of training camp with a hamstring injury, but when the lights turned on, he was ready to take center stage. He immediately proved his worth against the Jets. Moss caught 9 passes for 183 yards and a touchdown in a 38-14 victory.

"I was nervous before the game," Moss said. "I didn't know how much I was going to play or what might happen. I settled down after the first catch and the first hit. I don't think I ever was more anxious or more nervous. I didn't know how I would play."[lxi]

Through nine weeks, the Patriots were the most dominant team in NFL history. They won eight of those nine games by 17 points or more. Their closest game was a four-point victory over the Colts in Week

9. And then they traveled to Buffalo for Week 10, where Moss had the game of his life.

The Patriots scored on their first seven possessions. Moss caught 10 passes for 128 yards and a career-high 4 touchdowns. After the game, Belichick described Brady and Moss as "pretty good players." And then said nothing else on the subject.

"He put that humble pie on us. Actually, it was a humble pie casserole. It wasn't really a pie," Moss said. "Just being the coach that he is and not letting us get too ahead of ourselves, coming off a bye."[lxii]

Years later, though, Belichick was more effusive with his praise of Moss and what he was able to do during that special season.

"One of the smartest players I've ever coached. Certainly, the smartest receiver," Belichick said. "He taught me more about receiving and the passing game than by far anybody else. Randy had an energy that he brought to the team that was infectious."[lxiii]

The Patriots cruised through their first 15 games, not losing a single contest. In Week 16, New England traveled to Jersey to take on the Giants. Both teams had already clinched playoff berths but the Patriots were playing for immortality. Giants head coach Tom Coughlin decided to play all the team's starters against the Pats.

The game was incredibly hard-fought but the Pats ultimately won the game 38-35. Nevertheless, it would be the closest game the Patriots would play all season, and it would give the Giants confidence for a future meeting.

"It was a great performance. I'm really proud of my team" Coughlin said. "That's a team that's 16-0, we know we can play with them. All that stuff. Next morning at 5 o'clock I come into my office and I see the red light's on the phone. A voicemail. I pick up the phone and it's John Madden. He's saying, 'Tom, I just wanted to call. Because I want you to know that is the greatest thing that's happened to the NFL in the last 10 years.' He said, 'This is the National Football League— we don't not play our players. We owe a responsibility to our fans to perform every day. That's what you did. I'm just so proud to be a part of that. I'm so proud of what you've accomplished and what your team has accomplished.' He said, 'I'm very emotional right now. But I want you to know how I felt.' I played it for my team in our next team meeting. It was moving. Very moving."[lxiv]

With the victory, the Patriots became the first team in NFL history to complete a 16-game regular season undefeated. Moss set the single-season touchdown reception record with 23, breaking the mark held by Jerry Rice. He finished the year with 98 receptions for 1,493 yards.[lxv]

The Patriots had a bye for the first round of the playoffs and easily dispatched Jacksonville in the

Divisional Round. Waiting for them in the AFC Championship was the San Diego Chargers.

The Chargers had made an improbable run to the AFC Championship, knocking off the second-seeded Colts on the road. But winning that game cost them nearly their entire offense. Running back LaDainian Tomlinson hurt his knee and barely played in the game, while quarterback Phillip Rivers tore his ACL against the Colts but toughed it out and played the entire game against the Patriots.

The Patriots' offense looked lost at times. Brady was missing open receivers and Moss only caught one pass for 18 yards. In the end, though, they had just enough to beat the injured Chargers 21-12. They were now 18-0 and headed to Super Bowl XLII.

After having lost his previous two trips to conference championship games, Moss was finally on his way to a Super Bowl. The team that they would face was a familiar foe, the New York Giants.

The Giants came into the game as a 12-point underdog. They were a wild card team and the fifth seed in the NFC. They had somehow managed to win three-straight playoff games on the road in improbable fashion to make it to the Super Bowl, but now they would be facing a team on the verge of making history.

The Giants' defensive front harassed Brady all night long, ultimately sacking him five times. The game was a low-scoring defensive struggle for the first three quarters, with the Patriots up 7-3.

With 11 minutes remaining in the game, Giants quarterback Eli Manning found receiver David Tyree for a 5-yard touchdown pass to give the Giants the lead, 10-7. The Patriots answered right back when Brady found Moss for a 7-yard touchdown to retake the lead. It was Moss's first and only touchdown of the playoffs.

As time started to wind down, the Giants were driving. The Patriots appeared to have Manning sacked, but he did something improbable—he escaped the rush and lofted a pass deep down the field.

You are probably not a football fan if you are not aware of what happened next. Tyree jumped for the ball and made the seemingly impossible catch off the top of his helmet. The "helmet catch" was one of the greatest catches and plays in Super Bowl history and is still referenced to this day.

With less than 30 seconds remaining, Manning then hit Plaxico Burress in the end zone for the game-winning catch. And just like that, the Patriots' season was over. They lost the Super Bowl to the Giants 17-14 and their undefeated season went down in flames.

"They had the better team today," Moss said. "When things like that happen, all you can do is lick your wounds and come back next year."[lxvi]

The Patriots were that close to having only the second undefeated season in the history of the NFL, and it would have been the only time that a team won 19 games in a season. But in just one moment, it all slipped away from them.

"We had a great season," Moss continued. "We just didn't win the game. Tonight doesn't take away from anything we did over the course of the season. We had a great year. It is just unfortunate that tonight turned out the way it did."[lxvii]

The Hangover

As so often happens after a great team makes it all the way to the Super Bowl, there was a letdown. In the industry, this effect is sometimes referred to as a "hangover." And in this case, how could there not be? The Patriots had been on the verge of becoming the best team in NFL history. They were playing a team that by all accounts was inferior, and yet, they had everything slip through their hands. *Of course* there was going to be a letdown. The disappointment alone takes its toll, and the Patriots were simply not going to be perfect for a second straight season. But no one could have possibly foreseen what happened in the season opener.

Brady took a shot to the knee in the team's opening-day win over Kansas City. He was carted off the field and did not return for the remainder of the season. Brady, who was a staple of the Patriots dynasty, missed the entire year with a torn ACL.

Moss, whose reactionary comments were by this time as famous as his incredible talents on the field, had something to say about it. Whether you appreciated it or not, Randy Moss was going to tell it like he saw it.

"I don't really want to get into it, but me personally, I think it was dirty," Moss said of the hit on Brady. "Like I said, I didn't really see anything; I was running down the field. When I came back in [and watched it], it looked dirty to me. I've never been a dirty player. I honestly don't even know how to play dirty. I just play the game. Any time you see something like that, that looks foul, it looks dirty, it opens your eyes. So, me personally, it looked dirty."[lxviii]

But whether the hit was dirty or not did not matter. What mattered was that the Patriots were going to be without their starting quarterback for the entire season.

Brady was replaced by Matt Cassel, who had never started a professional game prior to Brady's injury. With their backup quarterback in place, the Patriots were still good—but not good *enough*.

They lost games to division foes Miami and the New York Jets, and they also lost to AFC powerhouse Pittsburgh, Indianapolis, and San Diego. The Patriots finished the year at 11-5, a solid record under the circumstances, but they just missed out on the playoffs.

Moss's numbers weren't nearly as good without Brady, but they were still respectable. He finished the year with 69 catches for 1,008 yards and 11 touchdowns. It was the ninth time in Moss's career that he had more than 1,000 receiving yards, and the eighth time he had more than 10 touchdowns in a season.^{lxix}

Prior to the 2008 season, Moss signed a new deal with the Patriots. He could have easily tested the free-agent waters and gotten significantly more money with another team, but he chose to stay in New England for three years and received $27 million for his loyalty.

"What Randy did for our team last year was outstanding," Patriots coach Bill Belichick said. "He is one of our most consistent, competitive and team-oriented players and it is undoubtedly a relationship we are excited to continue."^{lxx}

It appeared as though Moss had finally found a home in the NFL, but it would not last. A little more than two years after signing that contract, Moss would be on his way out of New England.

The 2009 season was one of transition for the Patriots. They lost four defensive starters who had won two or more Super Bowls with the team as well as a number of coaches who left for other jobs. Despite that, Tom Brady was back from his ACL injury.

The team played inconsistently all year long, something that had become uncharacteristic for the Patriots. They would win three in a row and then lose a game to an underdog. New England finished the year at 10-6, which was good enough to win the AFC East.

Moss's play, like the rest of the team, was wildly inconsistent. His catches, touchdowns, and yards were all up now that Brady was back, but it all came in bunches. He would have a 100-yard game, then follow that up with a two-catch game.

The Patriots hosted the Baltimore Ravens in the opening round of the playoffs. The Ravens were 9-7 and barely squeaked into the playoffs, but the Patriots came out completely flat and even the GOAT was struggling.

Brady turned the ball over three times in the first quarter. Before the crowd at Foxborough Stadium could finish their first hot dog, the Ravens were winning 24-0 and the Patriots were being booed off the field. The game was such a blowout early that Ravens quarterback Joe Flacco only threw for 34 yards in the game. The Ravens ended up winning 33-14.

"All of us that participated in the game are accountable for our performance," Belichick said, "and I don't think anybody felt very good about it, players, coaches, anybody."[lxxi]

Moss only caught five passes for 48 yards against a stingy Ravens defense. In four playoff games with the Patriots, Moss only caught one touchdown, and that was in the Super Bowl.

The Beginning of the End

Randy Moss was entering the final year of his contract with the New England Patriots. At the time, Moss was 33 years old and looking for the final payday of his illustrious career. But what Moss did not realize was that the Patriots didn't pay anyone, especially not a receiver of his advancing age. So, Moss entered the season with just that one year left and no new contract.

After the team's Week 1 victory over Cincinnati, Moss let his displeasure be known. Again, in a way that was not a part of the Patriots' way of doing things.

"I want to let [reporters] know, let the fans, the *real* fans of New England, know that I'm not here to cause any trouble, I'm here to play the last year out on my contract," Moss said. "I said time and time again before I signed my first contract here, I want to be in New England; it's a well-coached group here. I never said I wanted to leave New England, there are a lot of things that are being written or being said that have people looking at me in a negative light."

"I don't want to be in a negative light," Moss continued. "I want everybody to understand—you can print it; I don't care how you put it to ink—I want to be here with the Patriots. I love being here. I just think that, from a business standpoint, this will be my last year with the Patriots and I'm not retiring; I'm still going to play some football. I just want to get that off my chest. Understand that this is a business."[lxxii]

Moss had committed the cardinal sin in Patriot Land; he had told people outside of the organization what he was thinking. From that moment on, the writing was on the wall. Moss's time in New England was done.

After a Week 4 victory over the Miami Dolphins in which Moss did not catch a single pass, he was traded back to the Minnesota Vikings for a third-round draft pick. His three-plus seasons with the Patriots had been a great success for Moss, but he still fell short of his ultimate goal, winning a Super Bowl. Now, he was headed back to where it had all started.

"I've been traded before. I was more hurt when I left Minnesota the first time," Moss said. "I think when I got traded from New England, I feel it was more of an understanding. I've said time and time again. This is not football, man. It's a job; it's a business. When the fans of the game understand the business of the game, I think it'll be better for everyone."[lxxiii]

Moss started out well in Minnesota with 4 catches for 81 yards and a touchdown in a loss to the Jets, but that would be his only highlight. In his fourth game with Minnesota, Moss caught one pass for eight yards in a loss to the Patriots. After the game, he decided that he was no longer going to speak with the media.

"Well, I am going to go ahead and start this thing off," Moss said. "I am going to go ahead and say this—I said this a couple of weeks ago, but I got fined $25,000 for not talking to you all. Me, personally, I really don't care, but at the same time, I do answer questions throughout the week, and for the league to fine me $25,000 ... I am not going to answer any more questions for the rest of this year. If it is going to be an interview, I am going to conduct it. So, I will answer my own questions and ask myself the questions and give you the answers. So, from here on out, I am not answering any more questions the rest of this season. Enough said about that."

Moss continued, "Coach Belichick gave me an opportunity to be a part of something special and that is something I really take to heart. I actually salute Coach Belichick and his team for the success that they have had before me, during me and after me. So, I am actually stuck for words, just because there are a lot of memories here."[lxxiv]

The next day, the Vikings waived Moss, and this came less than a month after trading a third-round pick to get him. Moss's outspokenness had gotten him into trouble yet again, but you still could not ignore his talent. He was quickly claimed by the Tennessee Titans, who were 5-3 at the time. The Titans had quarterback Vince Young but lacked a true number-one receiver, and they hoped that Moss would be that for them.

"Timing is everything," Titans coach Jeff Fisher said. "I really think the quicker we get him on the field, the longer he's here, the more productive he'll be. We think that he can help us, and I'm looking forward to seeing him run under those deep balls. Randy's been a good teammate, and he's very popular. I think this is a great opportunity for him. It's a fresh start. We've got a great locker room. They'll accept him. I'm confident he'll accept his new teammates as well."[lxxv]

Despite that optimism, the acquisition of Moss was not fruitful for the Titans. He played in the team's final eight games, catching only six passes total and no touchdowns. The Titans were 1-7 in those games and missed the playoffs.

After the season ended, Moss was officially a free agent, but it seemed like he had very few options remaining. He had played for three different teams in 2010 with very little success. Finally, just as training camps opened, Moss decided to retire. There wasn't a long speech, nor was there a teary goodbye. Just a simple one-sentence goodbye from his agent.

"Randy has weighed his options and considered the offers and has decided to retire," Moss's agent, Joel Segal, said.[lxxvi]

Randy Moss left the game as one of the greatest receivers of all time. He held a number of major NFL receiver records, including most touchdown receptions in a season, most touchdown receptions by a rookie, most seasons with 17 or more touchdowns, most seasons with 10 or more touchdown receptions, fastest player to 5,000 receiving yards, and youngest player to reach 120 touchdown receptions.[lxxvii]

This would not be Moss's final act, however. After sitting out the entire 2011 season, Moss returned for the 2012 season. He signed a one-year deal to play for the San Francisco 49ers. Moss signed with the team after a one-day workout, with the team and head coach Jim Harbaugh throwing him the football.

"I'm not a free agent. I'm a guy straight off the couch, straight off the street," Moss said. "One thing I want the sports world to understand is the love and passion I have for football. It was a decision to get back in the game because I still love the game and think I can play at a high level. It was obvious they liked what they saw. I don't want to let them down."[lxxviii]

At his age and after spending a year on the couch, Moss had a respectable season for the 49ers. San Francisco ended the season at 11-4-1, winning the NFC West title and the second seed in the NFC. Moss had 28 receptions for 434 yards and 3 touchdowns. But his presence was just as important off the field as a mentor.

"It's about us, it's about the team," Harbaugh said. "And Randy, there's no evidence that he's concerned about 'The Guy' tag. He knows football. He knows the team that plays best is going to win the game. He's been about that."[lxxix]

Moss was back in the playoffs for what would be the final time of his career. The 49ers knocked off the Packers in the Divisional Round and took on the top-seeded Falcons in the NFC Championship.

Down 24-10 at the half, the 49ers' defense took over the game and did not allow a single point for the rest of the game. Meanwhile, the 49ers scored early in the fourth quarter to take a 28-24 lead, and that's how the game would end. Moss played a small role in both of the 49ers' playoff victories, catching only five passes combined in the two games.

But despite that, Moss was on his way to the Super Bowl for the second time in his career. He would have a front-row seat for the Harbaugh Bowl, as Jim was the coach of the 49ers and his older brother John was the coach of the Baltimore Ravens.

Baltimore took a huge lead early in the game, however, the 49ers charged back in the third quarter. But the Ravens were able to hold on for a three-point victory.

Again, Moss played a small role in his team's loss in the Super Bowl. He only had two catches.

For Moss, it would be the last time that he would ever step on an NFL field, at least as a player. He quietly retired and made the move into television.

In 2018, Moss took his place among the NFL greats as he was inducted into the Pro Football Hall of Fame.

"I'm all about family and putting smiles on people's faces. I've had a bumpy road and there's been a lot of people here to pray or help me through everything I've been through and I owed it to the people," Moss said.[lxxx]

And with that, the career of one of the greatest and most controversial receivers in NFL history came to a close.

But it was far from the end for Randy Moss. It would spark a new beginning for the outspoken legend, this time as a member of the media. How ironic that the opinionated commentary that so often got him into trouble as a player would ultimately become one of his greatest assets! Indeed, Moss would go on to become a much-loved and highly-respected NFL commentator. Nevertheless, he will also always be remembered as one of the greatest receivers of all time.

Chapter 4: Personal Life

Randy Moss's personal life has been just as controversial as his play on the field. Moss met Libby Offutt when the two were in high school. Offutt, who was white, and Moss started dating, which caused problems for them in the overtly racist Dupont High School. The two welcomed their first daughter, Sydney when Moss was a senior in high school. A few years later, they welcomed a son, Thaddeus.

Despite a somewhat tumultuous relationship, the two remained together for many years. Offutt would commute from her home in West Virginia to Minnesota while Moss was playing for the Vikings. The pair welcomed three more children: Senali, Montigo, and Sylee.

But after Moss's playing career ended, so did the troubled union with Offutt. Shortly after their breakup, Moss met Lydia Griffith. The two hit it off and had a daughter, Lourdes, together in 2014. In 2015, Moss and Griffith were married. She brought to Moss the stable personal life that he had always been looking for.

Moss's son, Thaddeus, became a football player himself. He started his college career at North Carolina State but transferred to LSU. In the College Football Playoffs Championship, he caught two touchdown passes from Joe Burrow to help the Tigers win the game. Thaddeus subsequently went undrafted, then signed as a free agent with Washington but was cut. He was later signed by Cincinnati but only played for their practice squad.

In retirement, Moss started looking around for something to do. He found his something in coaching. He started out by being a volunteer coach for his son's high school team, but that turned into something bigger for his home state.

Every summer, Moss returns to West Virginia on the former site of Dupont High School to hold a three-week clinic for the local kids. Moss is not just a name on the t-shirt for his clinic. He is there every day, working with these kids and teaching them about the game of football and about life off the field.

"When he first got here, they just wanted to be up close to him to say, 'Hey, I'm next to Randy Moss,'" Dupont principal Tommy Canterbury said. "But, then, I don't really believe they thought about, 'He's our coach.' They just like to be around him. Not because he was Randy Moss, but because of his personality. He was always upbeat."[lxxxi]

Moss's clinic helps these kids learn the game but it also shows them that it is possible to get out of West Virginia and make something of yourself in the wider world. It also helps them gain exposure to college coaches who otherwise would not have come to Rand, West Virginia.

"He would have been an excellent teacher," Canterbury said. "He would be as good a teacher as a football player. I really believe that. The kids knew he wanted to be there. You can't fool kids. They knew he really enjoyed it. They knew he was having fun and that was pretty cool to see."[lxxxii]

Despite his love/hate relationship with his home state, Moss still returns there as often as possible. Every Thanksgiving, he returns to donate turkeys to needy families. And when Dupont Middle School needed help with the football facilities, they knew who to call.

But they were not expecting that Moss would go all out. He donated money to help build new locker rooms for both home and visiting teams, but also a brand-new weight room and a player's lounge complete with big screen TVs and video games.

He also started the Randy Moss Foundation, whose goal is to help kids in need, whatever those needs may be.

Believe it or not, Moss is also an expert fisherman. Having grown up on the Kanawha River, which was just a few blocks from his house, fishing and swimming came naturally to Moss. He now hosts a yearly bass fishing event in Minnesota to raise money for charity.

Once he got off the field, Moss also headed right into the television studio. With his larger-than-life personality and outspoken opinions, he was the perfect fit. He started his career on the *Fox Pregame Show* in 2012, and then in 2016, he made the jump to ESPN.

While at ESPN, Moss has been a co-host of *Sunday NFL Countdown* and *Monday Night Countdown*. In 2022, Moss finally left *Monday Night Countdown* and currently appears on ESPN's Sunday show where he remains one of their most popular commentators.

Randy Moss has made good. He started as a kid from Rand, West Virginia, and is now a Hall-of-Famer and a beloved television personality. Not bad for a dropout of "Rand University."

Chapter 5: Legacy

Whenever there is a debate over who is the greatest receiver of all time, Randy Moss is in the conversation. Moss is fifth all-time in receiving yards, 15th all-time in receptions, and second in receiving touchdowns.

Moss was first-team All-Pro four times in his career and played in the Pro Bowl six times. He was also the Offensive Rookie of the Year and was named to the Hall of Fame's All-2000 Team.

There are perhaps two stains on Moss's legacy that hurt his argument for being the GOAT. One is the negative media attention that he has attracted over the years. Yes, he was guilty of some youthful indiscretions, and we must concede that his behavior off the field has not been entirely spotless. Furthermore, his passion for the game and blunt outspokenness sometimes resulted in the venting of frustrations in ways that were not well received. But it is also fair to say that Moss has often been judged unfairly and over harshly. He has always been a larger-than-life personality that has had to deal with the pressures of being perpetually "under the microscope." But to know Randy Moss personally is to know a kind, generous, compassionate leader and loyal friend. He is someone who clearly deserves the respect and recognition of the industry he has devoted his life to.

The other argument is his lack of a Super Bowl win. Jerry Rice, the other possible greatest receiver of all time, has three Super Bowl wins. Moss was 0-2 in his two tries at winning a ring. But despite all that, Moss passes the eye test. When he was at his best, there was no more dominant receiver in the history of the NFL. It was not necessarily about how many balls he caught but the way he did it. He could out-jump and outrun any defensive back. It was a thing of beauty to watch.

All in all, Randy Moss's career is as complicated as the man himself. When he was in his prime, there was simply no one better. In 2007, he had the best season of any receiver in the history of the NFL. Put together with a great quarterback and coach, and there was no stopping him. He truly is one of the greats, and no one can take that away from him.

Final Word/About the Author

I was born and raised in Norwalk, Connecticut. Growing up, I could often be found spending many nights watching basketball, soccer, and football matches with my father in the family living room. I love sports and everything that sports can embody. I believe that sports are one of the most genuine forms of competition, heart, and determination. I write my works to learn more about influential athletes in the hopes that from my writing, you the reader can walk away inspired to put in an equal if not greater amount of hard work and perseverance to pursue your goals. If you enjoyed *Randy Moss: The Inspiring Story of One of Football's Star Wide Receivers,* please leave a review! Also, you can read more of my works on *David Ortiz, Cody Bellinger, Alex Bregman, Francisco Lindor, Shohei Ohtani, Ronald Acuna Jr., Javier Baez, Jose Altuve, Christian Yelich, Max Scherzer, Mookie Betts, Pete Alonso, Clayton Kershaw, Mike Trout, Bryce Harper, Jackie Robinson, Justin Verlander,*

Derek Jeter, Ichiro Suzuki, Ken Griffey Jr., Babe Ruth, Aaron Judge, Novak Djokovic, Roger Federer, Rafael Nadal, Serena Williams, Naomi Osaka, Coco Gauff, Baker Mayfield, George Kittle, Matt Ryan, Matthew Stafford, Eli Manning, Khalil Mack, Davante Adams, Terry Bradshaw, Jimmy Garoppolo, Philip Rivers, Von Miller, Aaron Donald, Joey Bosa, Josh Allen, Mike Evans, Joe Burrow, Carson Wentz Adam Thielen, Stefon Diggs, Lamar Jackson, Dak Prescott, Patrick Mahomes, Odell Beckham Jr., J.J. Watt, Colin Kaepernick, Aaron Rodgers, Tom Brady, Russell Wilson, Peyton Manning, Drew Brees, Calvin Johnson, Brett Favre, Rob Gronkowski, Andrew Luck, Richard Sherman, Bill Belichick, Candace Parker, Skylar Diggins-Smith, A'ja Wilson, Lisa Leslie, Sue Bird, Diana Taurasi, Julius Erving, Clyde Drexler, John Havlicek, Oscar Robertson, Ja Morant, Gary Payton, Khris Middleton, Michael Porter Jr., Julius Randle, Jrue Holiday, Domantas Sabonis, Mike Conley Jr., Jerry West, Dikembe Mutombo, Fred

VanVleet, Jamal Murray, Zion Williamson, Brandon Ingram, Jaylen Brown, Charles Barkley, Trae Young, Andre Drummond, JJ Redick, DeMarcus Cousins, Wilt Chamberlain, Bradley Beal, Rudy Gobert, Aaron Gordon, Kristaps Porzingis, Nikola Vucevic, Andre Iguodala, Devin Booker, John Stockton, Jeremy Lin, Chris Paul, Pascal Siakam, Jayson Tatum, Gordon Hayward, Nikola Jokic, Bill Russell, Victor Oladipo, Luka Doncic, Ben Simmons, Shaquille O'Neal, Joel Embiid, Donovan Mitchell, Damian Lillard, Giannis Antetokounmpo, Chris Bosh, Kemba Walker, Isaiah Thomas, DeMar DeRozan, Amar'e Stoudemire, Al Horford, Yao Ming, Marc Gasol, Draymond Green, Kawhi Leonard, Dwyane Wade, Ray Allen, Pau Gasol, Dirk Nowitzki, Jimmy Butler, Paul Pierce, Manu Ginobili, Pete Maravich, Larry Bird, Kyle Lowry, Jason Kidd, David Robinson, LaMarcus Aldridge, Derrick Rose, Paul George, Kevin Garnett, Michael Jordan, LeBron James, Kyrie Irving, Klay Thompson, Stephen Curry, Kevin Durant, Russell Westbrook,

Chris Paul, Blake Griffin, Kobe Bryant, Anthony Davis, Joakim Noah, Scottie Pippen, Carmelo Anthony, Kevin Love, Grant Hill, Tracy McGrady, Vince Carter, Patrick Ewing, Karl Malone, Tony Parker, Allen Iverson, Hakeem Olajuwon, Reggie Miller, Michael Carter-Williams, James Harden, John Wall, Tim Duncan, Steve Nash, Gregg Popovich, Pat Riley, John Wooden, Steve Kerr, Brad Stevens, Red Auerbach, Doc Rivers, Erik Spoelstra, Mike D'Antoni, and *Phil Jackson* in the Kindle Store. If you love football, check out my website at claytongeoffreys.com to join my exclusive list where I let you know about my latest books and give you lots of goodies.

Like what you read? Please leave a review!

I write because I love sharing the stories of influential athletes like Randy Moss with fantastic readers like you. My readers inspire me to write more so please do not hesitate to let me know what you thought by leaving a review! If you love books on life, sports, or productivity, check out my website at claytongeoffreys.com to join my exclusive list where I let you know about my latest books. Aside from being the first to hear about my latest releases, you can also download a free copy of *33 Life Lessons: Success Principles, Career Advice & Habits of Successful People*. See you there!

Clayton

References

[i] "Top 10 Hungriest States in the US." Friends Committee on National Legislation. Oct. 11, 2022. Web.

[ii] Weir, Josh. "A Day with Dad...and Randy Moss." The Canton Repository. June 23, 2018.

[iii] "Randy Moss: Hometown." NBCSports.Com. Nov. 14, 2012. Web.

[iv] "Rand University." Daisy, Marquis. ESPN Studios. 2014.

[v] "Randy Moss: Hometown." NBCSports.Com. Nov. 14, 2012. Web.

[vi] Rodrick, Stephen. "Two for One." ESPN The Magazine. July 12, 1999.

[vii] Askeland, Kevin. "Randy Moss, Cris Carter Lead Top 25 Wide Receivers in High School Football History." MaxPreps.Com. Oct. 10, 2019. Web.

[viii] Rodrick, Stephen. "Two for One." ESPN The Magazine. July 12, 1999.

[ix] MacMullan, Jackie. "Moss's Blessing, and Curse." The Boston Globe. Jan. 20, 2008.

[x] "Rand University." Daisy, Marquis. ESPN Studios. 2014.

[xi] MacMullan, Jackie. "Moss's Blessing, and Curse." The Boston Globe. Jan. 20, 2008.

[xii] "Randy Moss: Hometown." NBCSports.Com. Nov. 14, 2012. Web.

[xiii] Price, SL. "Cut Off From the Herd: Randy Moss's Journey as Marshall's Biggest Star." Sports Illustrated. Nov. 12, 2014.

[xiv] MacMullan, Jackie. "Moss's Blessing, and Curse." The Boston Globe. Jan. 20, 2008.

[xv] MacMullan, Jackie. "Moss's Blessing, and Curse." The Boston Globe. Jan. 20, 2008.

[xvi] "Rand University." Daisy, Marquis. ESPN Studios. 2014.

[xvii] MacMullan, Jackie. "Moss's Blessing, and Curse." The Boston Globe. Jan. 20, 2008.

[xviii] MacMullan, Jackie. "Moss's Blessing, and Curse." The Boston Globe. Jan. 20, 2008.

[xix] "Rand University." Daisy, Marquis. ESPN Studios. 2014.

[xx] "Rand University." Daisy, Marquis. ESPN Studios. 2014.

[xxi] "Rand University." Daisy, Marquis. ESPN Studios. 2014.

[xxii] "Rand University." Daisy, Marquis. ESPN Studios. 2014.

[xxiii] "Plane Crash Devastates Marshall University Football Team." History.Com. Nov, 12, 2020. Web.

[xxiv] Redd, Derek. "Randy Moss: The Marshall Years." The Herald Dispatch. Aug. 2, 2018.

[xxv] Redd, Derek. "Randy Moss: The Marshall Years." The Herald Dispatch. Aug. 2, 2018.

[xxvi] Couch, Greg. "A Brief Glimpse of the Randy Moss We Don't Know." Bleacher Report. June 9, 2015.

[xxvii] "Randy Moss." American Football Database. 2020. Web.

[xxviii] Redd, Derek. "Randy Moss: The Marshall Years." The Herald Dispatch. Aug. 2, 2018.

[xxix] Rothschild, Richard. "Marshall Routs Montana to Capture NCAA 1AA Title." Chicago Tribune. Dec. 22, 1996.

[xxx] "Rand University." Daisy, Marquis. ESPN Studios. 2014.

[xxxi] "Rand University." Daisy, Marquis. ESPN Studios. 2014.

[xxxii] "Rand University." Daisy, Marquis. ESPN Studios. 2014.

[xxxiii] Price, SL. "Cut Off From the Herd: Randy Moss's Journey as Marshall's Biggest Star." Sports Illustrated. Nov. 12, 2014. an

[xxxiv] "Motor City Bowl: Mississippi Captures Wild One." New York Times. Dec. 27, 1997.

[xxxv] "Marshall's Moss to Miss Combine." New York Times. Feb. 7, 1998.

[xxxvi] "Rand University." Daisy, Marquis. ESPN Studios. 2014.

[xxxvii] Peters, Craig. "The Drafting of Randy Moss Changed NFL Landscape 20 Years Ago." Vikings.Com. April 18, 2018. Web.

[xxxviii] Stroud, Rick. "Bucs CB Floyd Young VS Vikings Receivers." Tampa Bay Times Oct. 6, 1998.

[xxxix] Carter, Bob. "Moss Gobbles up Cowboys." ESPN.Com. Nov. 27, 1998. Web.

[xl] "Randy Moss 1998 Game Log" Pro-Football Reference. Com. 2020. Web.

[xli] Ikic, Adnan. "A Tale of Two Andersons and One NFC Championship Game." The Falconholic.Com. Aug. 30, 2018. Web.

[xlii] Steele, David. "For Dennis Green Loss by '98 Vikings Altered Coaching Legacy." The Sporting News. July 24, 2016.

[xliii] Davis, Nate. "Super Bowl Stumble: The 16 Best NFL Teams of All-Time That Didn't Reach Super Sunday." USA Today. Feb. 3, 2023.

[xliv] "Randy Moss 1999 Game Logs." Pro-Football Reference.Com. 2020. Web.

[xlv] Britton, Tim. "'We Just Annihilated Them': Revisiting the 2000 Giants' NFC Title Game Rout." The Athletic. Jan. 29, 2021.

[xlvi] Jurgens, Roy. "Moss Lands a $75-million Deal." Los Angeles Times. July 26, 2001.

[xlvii] "Randy Moss 2001 Game Logs." Pro-Football Reference.Com. 2020. Web.

[xlviii] Ekstrom, Sam. "Randy Moss Gets Emotional When Talking About Dennis Green." Zonecoverage.Com. Aug. 2, 2018. Web.

[xlix] "'Randy Ratio' Gone, Vikings Pleased with Moss's Leadership."

ESPN.Com. Aug. 16, 2003. Web.

[l] Maske, Mark. "Vikings Agree to Trade Moss to the Raiders." Washington Post. Feb. 24, 2005.

[li] "Randy Moss 2002 Game Log." Pro-Football Reference.Com. 2020. Web.

[lii] "'Randy Ratio' Gone, Vikings Pleased with Moss's Leadership." ESPN.Com. Aug. 16, 2003. Web.

[liii] "Randy Moss 2003 Game Logs." Pro-Football Reference.Com. 2020. Web.

[liv] "Moss's Early Exit Irks Teammates, Coaches." ESPN.Com. Jan. 6, 2005. Web.

[lv] "Moss's Early Exit Irks Teammates, Coaches." ESPN.Com. Jan. 6, 2005. Web.

[lvi] "Vikings on way to Philly After Stunning Packers." ESPN.Com. Jan. 9, 2005. Web.

[lvii] "Eagles Outplay Self-Destructing Vikings." ESPN.Com. Jan. 16, 2005. Web.

[lviii] Maske, Mark. "Vikings Agree to Trade Moss to the Raiders." Washington Post. Feb. 24, 2005.

[lix] "Unhappy at Work? Moss Says Mood Affecting Play." ESPN.Com. Nov. 14, 2006. Web.

[lx] "Raiders Trade Moss to Patriots for 4th Round Pick." ESPN.Com. April 29, 2007. Web.

[lxi] "Moss Has Huge Day." ESPN.Com. Sept. 10, 2007. Web.

[lxii] "Patriots Improve to 10-0 After Scoring on First Seven Possessions." ESPN.Com. Nov. 19, 2007.

[lxiii] McKenna, Henry. "Bill Belichick Says Randy Moss Taught Him More About the Passing Game Than Anyone." USA Today. Dec. 21, 2019.

[lxiv] Citak, Matt. "15-Year Anniversary of 'Paradoxical' Giants vs. Patriots Finale." Giants.Com. Dec. 28, 2022. Web.

[lxv] "Randy Moss 2007 Game Logs." Pro-Football Reference.Com. 2020. Web.

[lxvi] Seeholzer, Dan. "Moss Misses His Moment." Pioneer Press. Feb. 3, 2008.

[lxvii] Seeholzer, Dan. "Moss Misses His Moment." Pioneer Press. Feb. 3, 2008.

[lxviii] Reiss, Mike. "Randy Moss on 'Dirty' Play." Boston.Com. Sept. 7, 2008. Web.

[lxix] "Randy Moss 2008 Game Log." Pro-Football Reference.Com. 2020. Web.

[lxx] "All-Pro WR Moss Gets Three-Year Deal to Stay with the Patriots." ESPN.Com. March 3, 2008. Web.

[lxxi] "Ravens Fast Starts Puts Pats on Heels, Out of Playoffs." ESPN.Com.

January 10, 2010. Web.

[lxxii] Rogers, Dexter. "Randy Moss Traded to the Minnesota Vikings: Was Race A Factor?" Bleacher Report. Oct. 6, 2010.

[lxxiii] Reiss, Mike. "Bill Belichick: Combination of Factors'" ESPN.Com. Oct. 7, 2010. Web.

[lxxiv] Rogers, Dexter. "Randy Moss Cut by the Minnesota Vikings." Bleacher Report. Nov. 1, 2010.

[lxxv] "Titans Claim Randy Moss." ESPN.Com. Nov. 3, 2010. Web.

[lxxvi] "Randy Moss, 34, Hangs Up his Cleats." ESPN.Com. Aug. 1, 2011. Web.

[lxxvii] Young, Aaron. "Randy Moss: Future Hall of Famer Retires After 13 Seasons." Bleacher Report. Aug. 1, 2011.

[lxxviii] "49ers, Moss Agree to 1-Year Deal." ESPN.Com. March 12, 2012. Web.

[lxxix] Williams, Doug. "Moss Making Positive Impact on 49ers Offense." NBC Sports.Com. Oct. 30, 2012. Web.

[lxxx] "Randy Moss Officially Inducted Into Hall of Fame." CBS Sports.Com. Aug. 6, 2018. Web.

[lxxxi] "Randy Moss: Hometown." NBCSports.Com. Nov. 14, 2012. Web.

[lxxxii] "Randy Moss: Hometown." NBCSports.Com. Nov. 14, 2012. Web.

a poem, Randy
          moss
is not lost
~good carrer
did not bear
~God Bless ~~Ra~~
Randy ~~moss~~
          moss

          J

Made in the USA
Monee, IL
29 September 2023

43672024R00075